PRACTICALLY IN SHADOW

Plaster powder, powder paint, polythene, Sellotape, cellophane, florist foam,
bath bombs, nail varnish, thread

1200 x 1540 x 830 cm

by Karla Black

for the Institute of Contemporary Art
University of Pennsylvania, Philadelphia
April 24 - July 28, 2013

AMY SADAO
Daniel W. Dietrich, II Director at ICA

On behalf of ICA, I extend my thanks to Karla Black for transforming our galleries with an awe-inspiring sculpture. Thanks as well to her assistants Ronnie Black and Susie Simmons.

ICA's Assistant Curator Kate Kraczon arrived at ICA five years ago with the idea of presenting Karla Black's work. We are awed and grateful that she made this extraordinary project possible. The exhibition underscores the way in which she exemplifies our curatorial commitment to artists, and to the presentation of new works.

The excellence of ICA's program is flow from contributions by and the inspiration of our Chief Curator Ingrid Schaffner and Director of Curatorial Affairs Robert Chaney. ICA is renowned for its ambitious installations, *Karla Black* is the most recent example of the work of Associate Registrar Dana Hanmer, Chief Preparator & Building Administrator Paul Swenbeck and the extraordinary ICA installation crew of David Bruce, Thom Lessner, Isaac Lin, Preston Link, Jacob Lunderby, Patrick Maguire, Dietrich Meyer, Raul Romero, and Sophie White. Everything in the department runs smoothly because of our Curatorial Administrative Assistant Dana Fedeli, and Curatorial Intern Ella Cohen.

For his vision of publications as an extension of our exhibition practice, I thank Associate Curator Anthony Elms. Likewise, Dorothy A. & Stephen R. Weber (CHE'60) Program Curator Alex Klein, with Spiegel Fellow Grace Ambrose and Program Technician/Visitor Service Manager William Hidalgo enable conversation around the ideas circulating at ICA and result in a stellar selection of public events. I thank William, as well as Larry Rosen, for extending our public welcome to all ICA visitors. In the time between the exhibition and this catalogue's publication, we bid farewell to two staff members whose contributions to both this project and countless others continue to change ICA for the better. I offer my thanks to Christianna Miller, Major Gifts Officer and Jennifer Burris, Whitney-Lauder Curatorial Fellow.

Every new program requires new outreach and development strategies. ICA is lucky to have the capable experience of Jill Katz, Marketing and Communications Director; Editor-at-Large Rachel Pastan; and the Development team of Samantha Gibb, Jeffrey Bussmann, and Jessica Scipione. As the museum's Administrative Coordinator as well as my assistant Eliza Coviello works alongside our Business Administrator Shannon Freitas to shape ICA's inner workings enabling every new challenge for the museum, the artists, and our visitors. Their tireless efforts make our presentations a reality.

ICA is grateful to Julie L. & Lawrence J. Bernstein; Carol T. & John G. Finley; Kirk Kirkpatrick; Marjorie E. & Michael J. Levine; and Josephine M. & Christopher C. Schlank for their generous support of this exhibition. We thank Galerie Gisela Capitain—Gisela Capitain and Dorothee Sorge—for in-kind support.

In conclusion, at the University of Pennsylvania, I thank Board President Andie Lapore, the ICA's Board of Overseers as well as President Amy Gutmann and Provost Vincent Price for their unflagging support of ICA's commitment to new and compelling contemporary art.

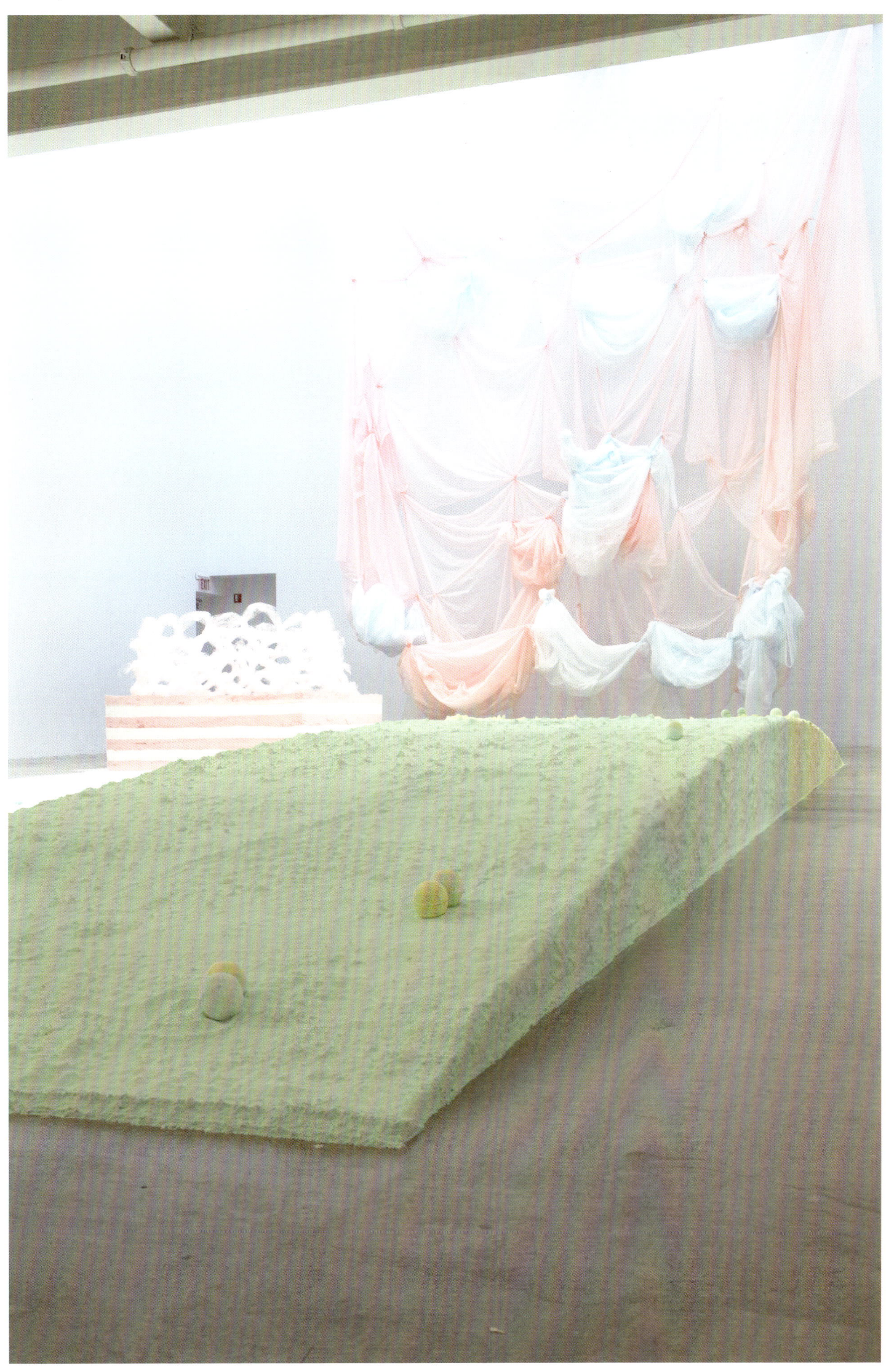

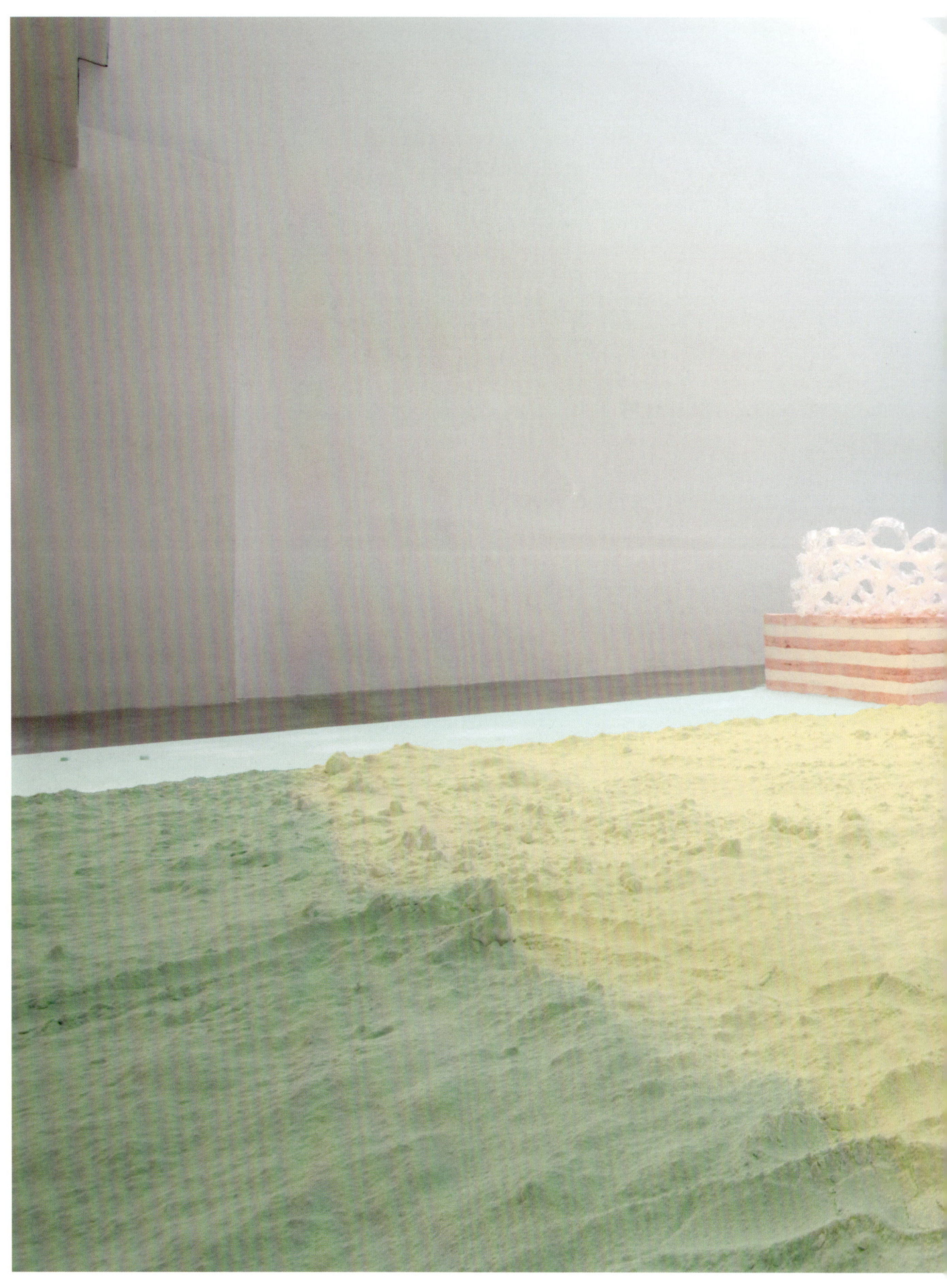

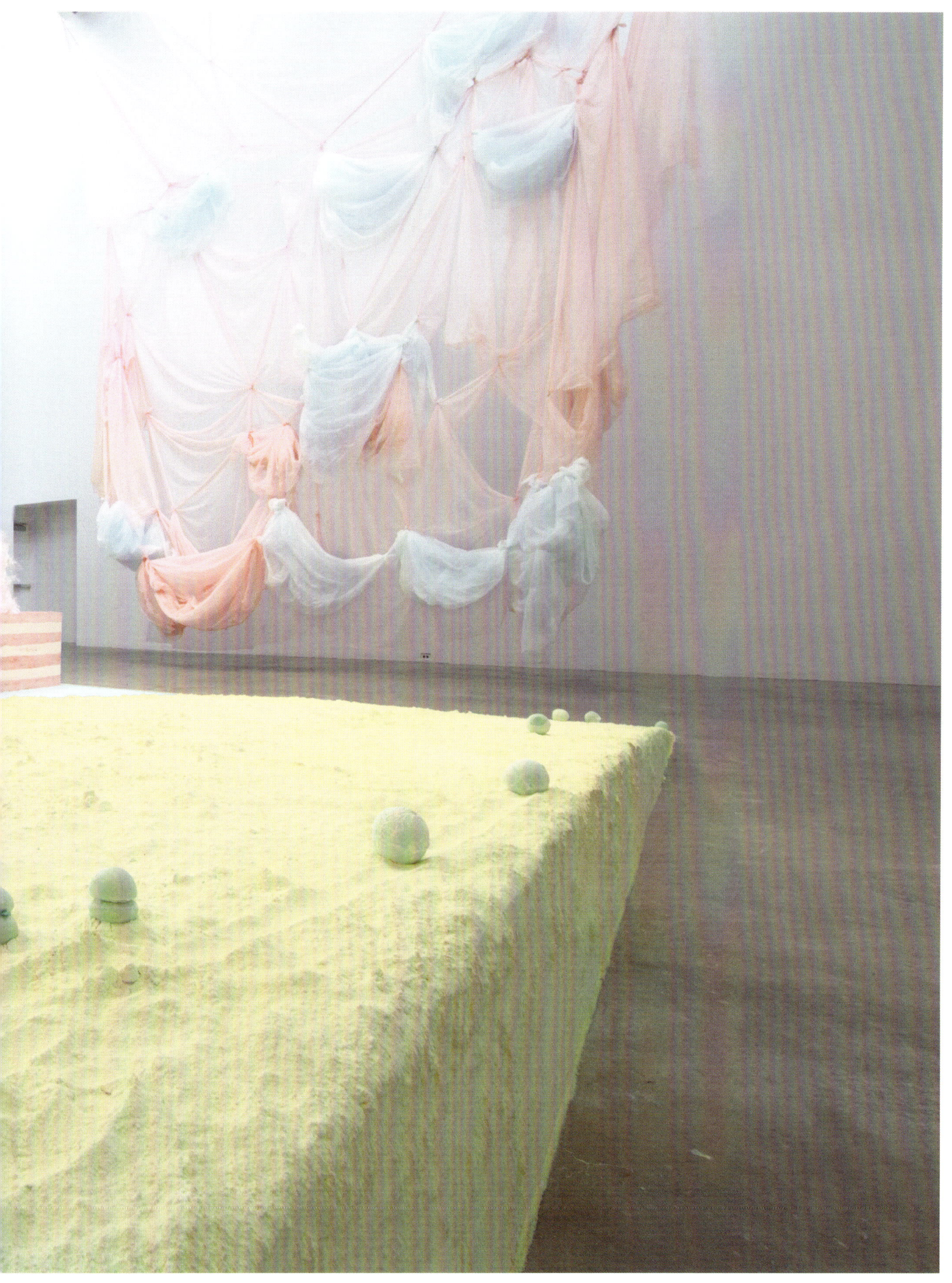

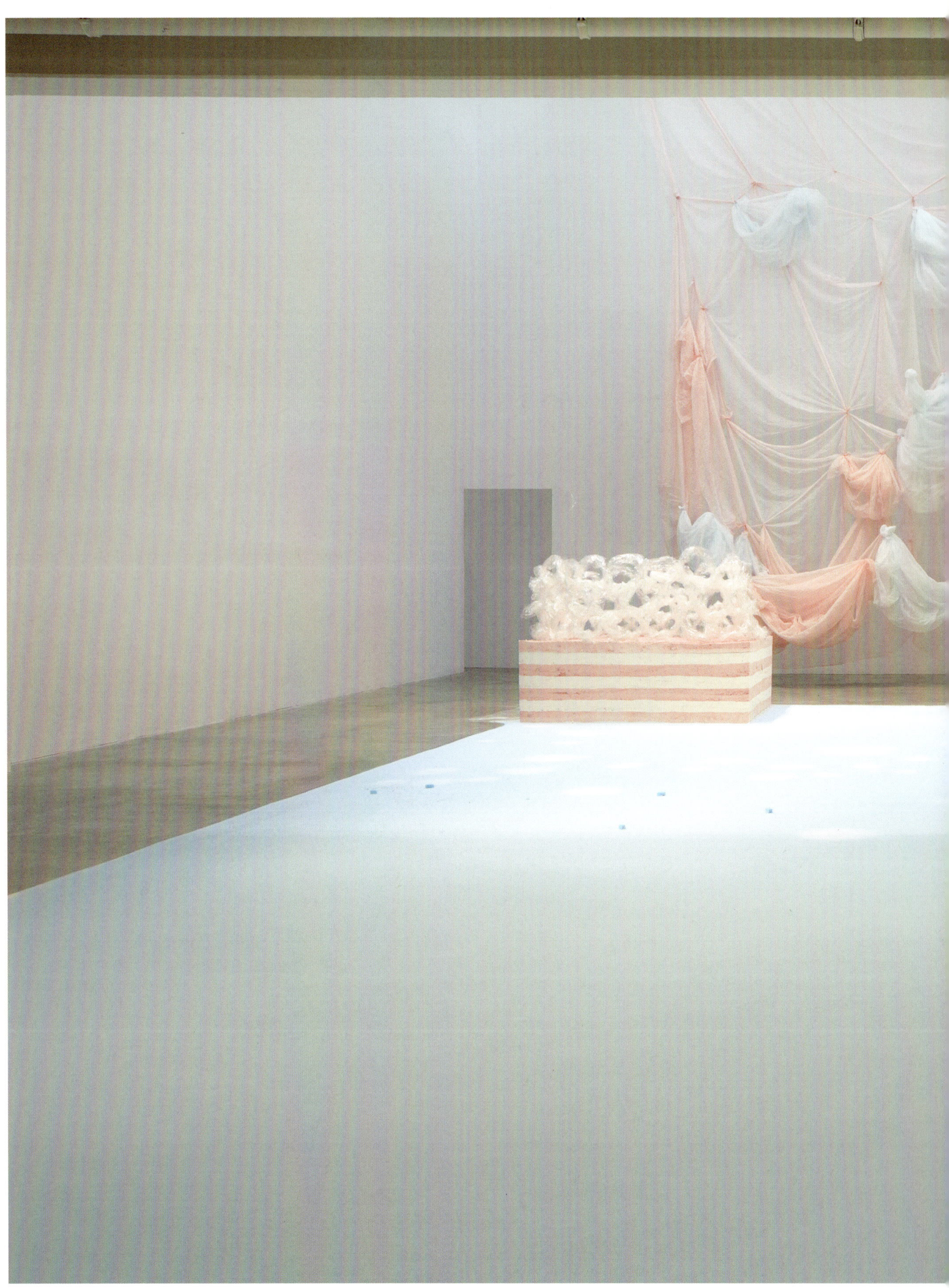

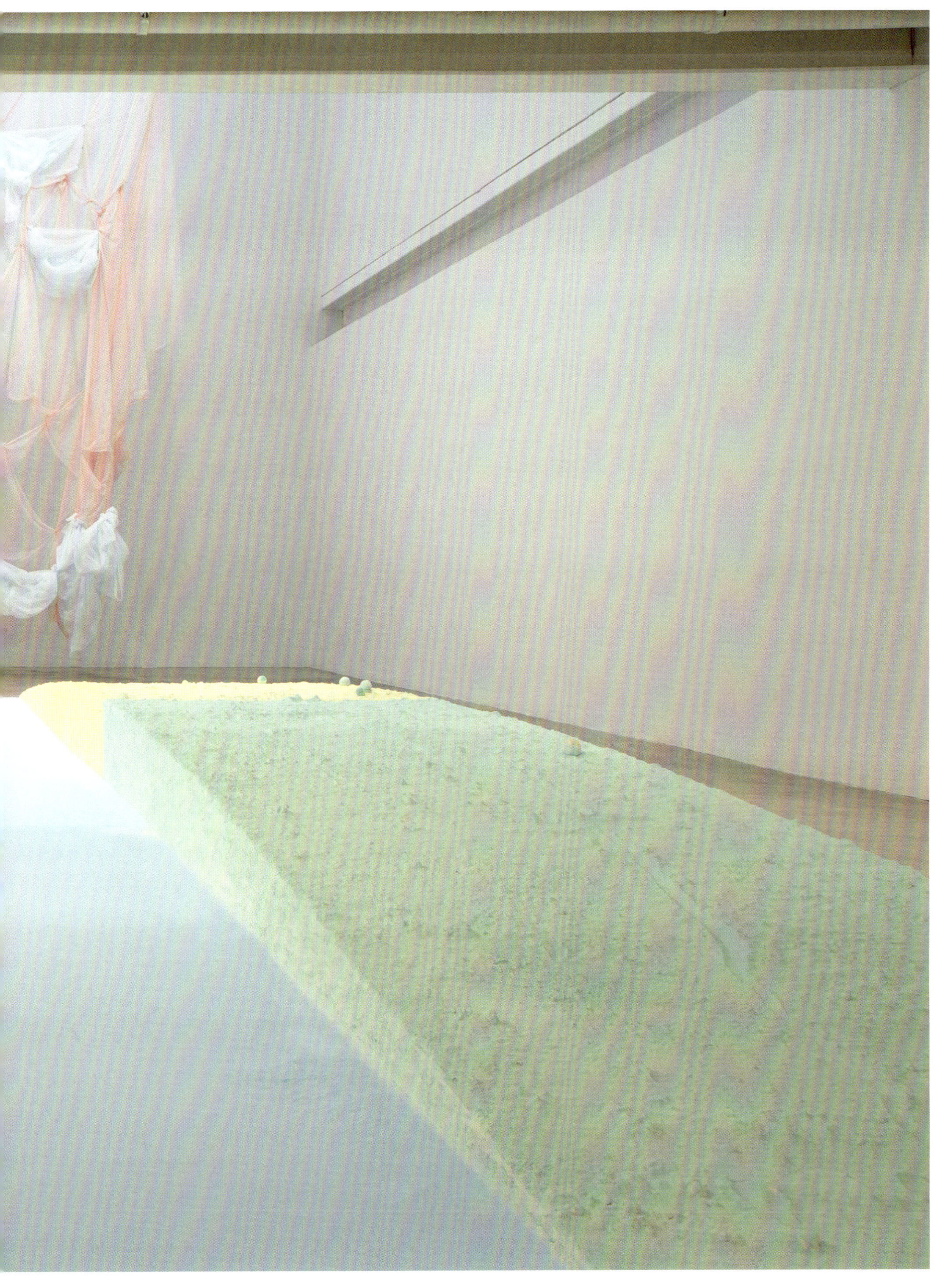

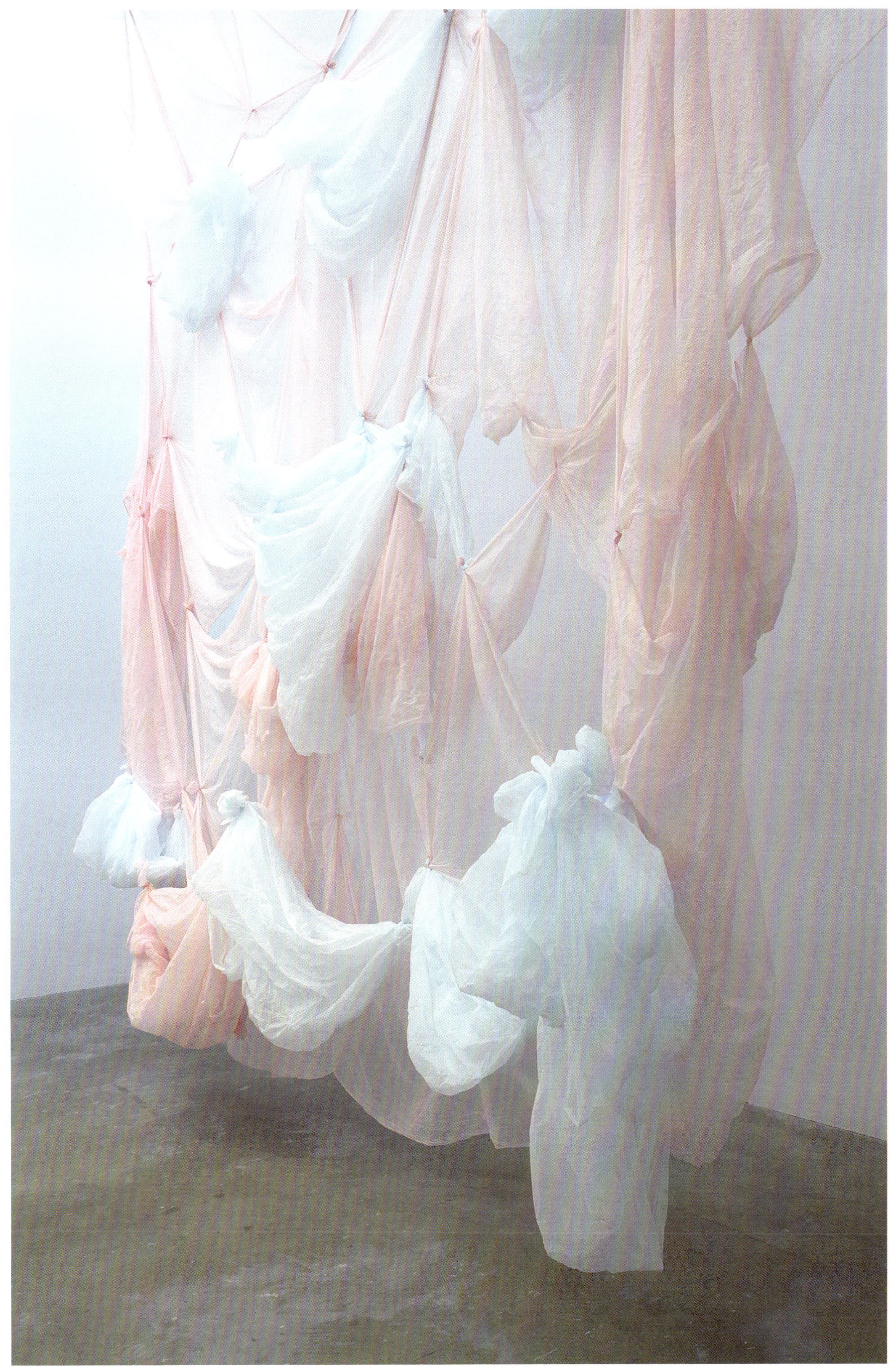

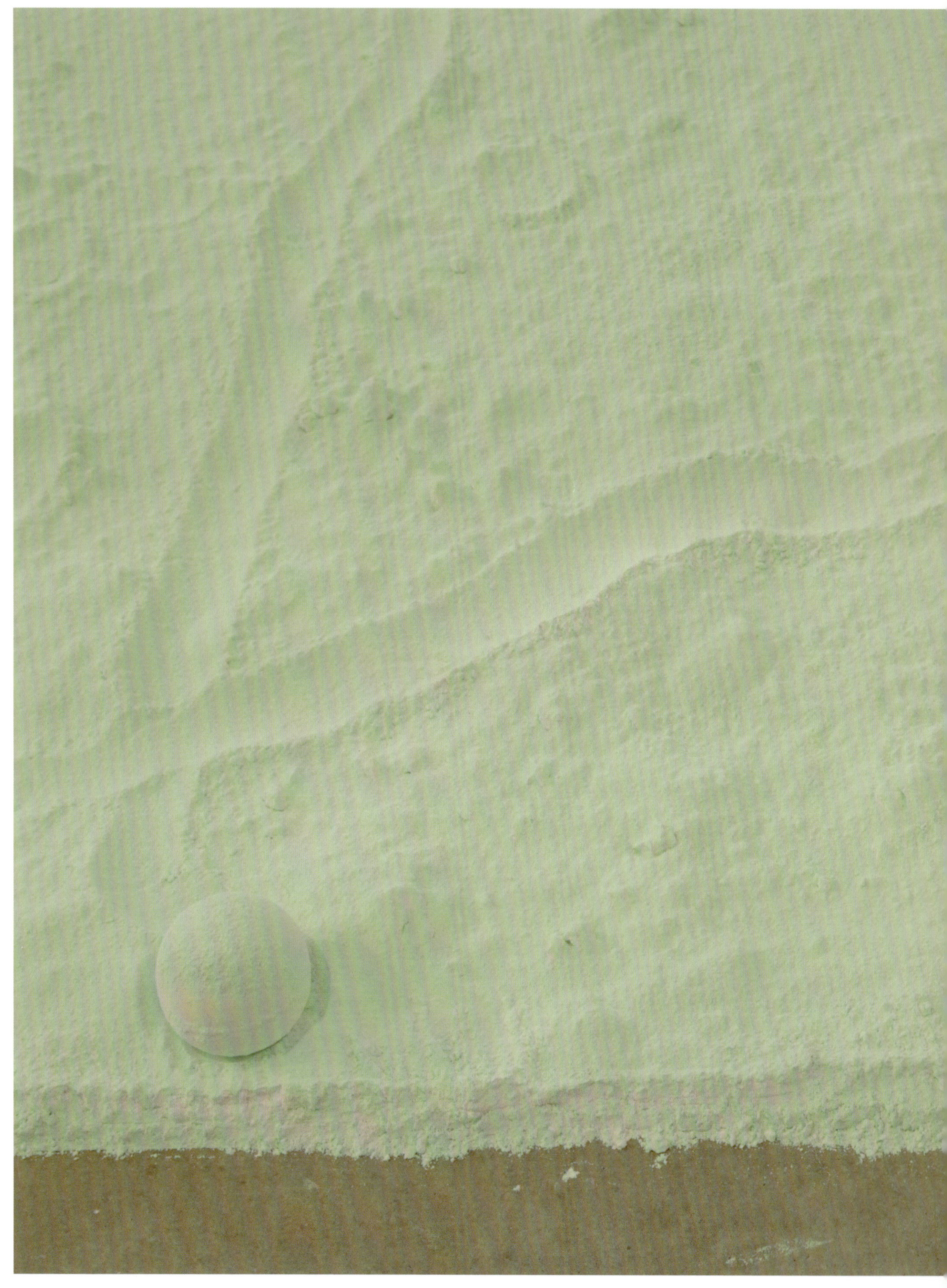

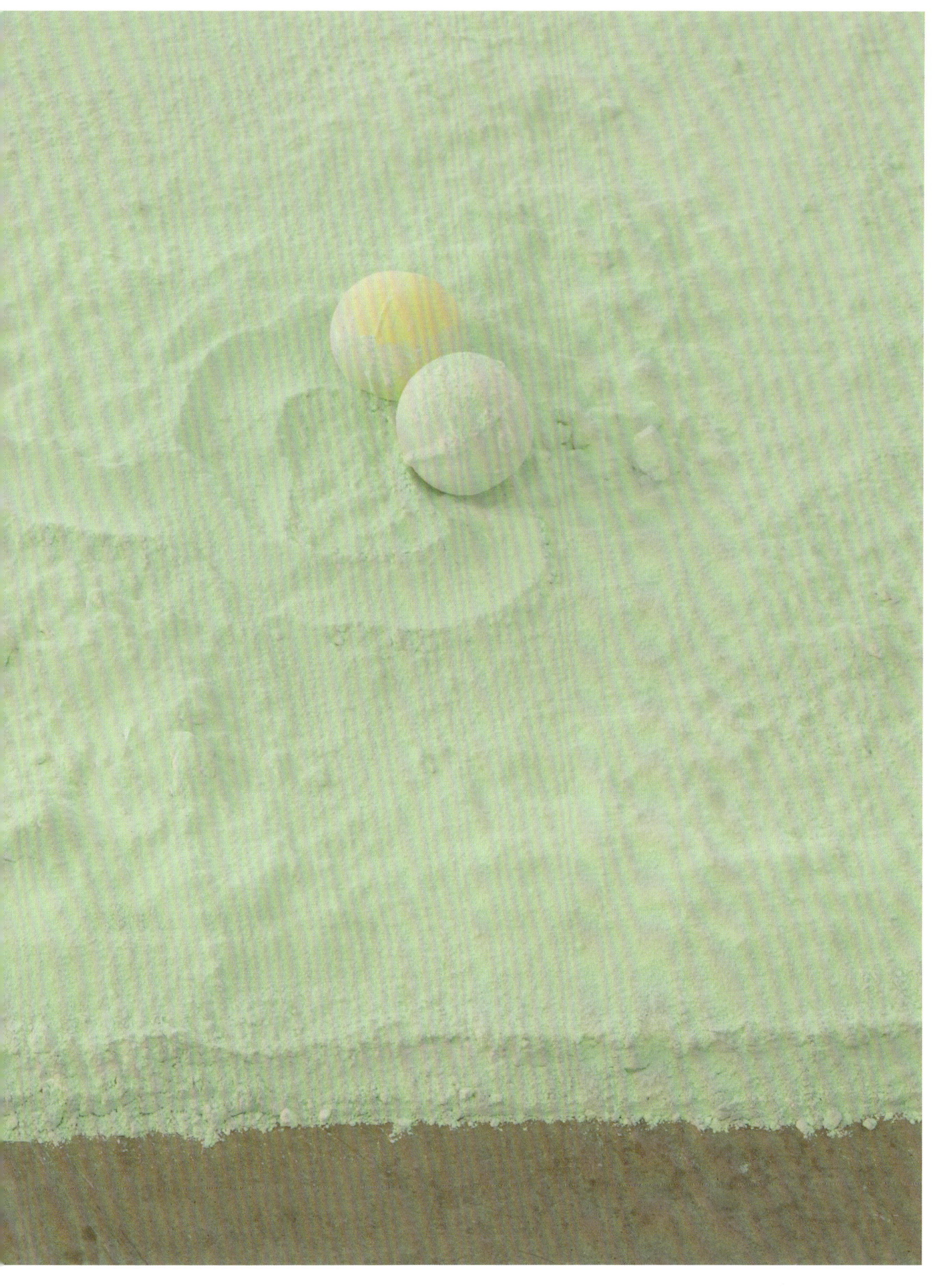

DEFIANTLY IMPERMANENT

Kate Kraczon

The "almost" pervades Karla Black's practice. [1] Large-scale, site-specific sculptures composed of amorphous yet everyday materials—from dirt, chalk, and dough to the powders, sprays, and gooey substances we use to coat our bodies—her work reacts to the light and space of each site with a sense of play and indeterminacy. The hues are "almost colors": pale blues and pinks, pastel greens and yellows, primary shades softened by the addition of white. The forms are "only just": precarious shapes in malleable materials—crumpled paper, translucent cellophane—structures that seem to be on the brink of collapse. Her approach is "almost purely formal": dominated by color, line, and shape but evoking a visceral, nearly tactile response. *Almost* gendered, her sculptures incorporate materials deemed ephemeral and unstable, transparent and delicate, though the feminine associations many of these substances produce are deflected through the machismo of mass and repetition. When she paints hundreds of dots of nail varnish on a cellophane sculpture, or covers a 150-square-foot space with pink powder, the sheer quantity of color and material resists a simple reading. The work is not fixed by the cultural connotations of these products but how they appear once Black recodes them as artistic materials. She chooses them for the pleasure she finds in their color, texture, weight, and shimmer, producing engulfing, multi-sensory environments that are, in Black's words, "almost painting, almost installation, almost performance art." [2]

Black's insistence that the work alludes to nothing beyond its materiality and the labor that produced it—that there is no narrative within the gallery-size sculptures—echoes claims made in the 1960s. Post-Minimalism's supple materials and bodily references are clearly traceable within Black's work. Her manipulation of pliable and powdered matter and her skilled deployment of gravity recall Barry Le Va's distributions, notably his use of flour in *Six Blown Lines* (1969). Robert Morris's writings on the unpredictable formal resolutions that these actions produce, elaborated in his 1968 essay "Anti-Form," are similarly conjured: "Random piling, loose stacking, hanging, give passing form to the material." [3] Eva Hesse is another dominant presence. Hesse's levitating ropes of latex and resin and the hanging scrims of *Contingent* (1969) share a formal and material sensibility with Black's work and project a similarly defiant impermanence. Yet this physical impermanence in Black's sculptures is reluctant. Her works' gradual decomposition over time has been accepted by the artist as an unavoidable, if undesirable, result of the materials she uses.

There is an underlying aggression in Black's treatment of these materials, a compulsion to oppose formlessness: cellophane is twisted, paper bent and balanced, powder packed into specific shapes, processes she has described as a "repression of materials." [4] The works are scattered with marks that indicate movement—from drips of nail polish to balls that seem to have been rolled or thrown—but these allusions to motion have been carefully composed. The randomness and chance that Morris refers to is, in Black's work, countered with defined borders. Oscillating between action and editing, she allows materials to slump and spread but "tidies" the lines of these large geometric segments of color, suggesting not just the anti-form of the 1960s but the hard boundaries of color-field painting.

Black has spoken of her desire to move an understanding of formlessness away from the abject and towards beauty through her use of color. Often erroneously conflated, the terms *formlessness* and *abjection* within art criticism are commonly associated with French surrealist and philosopher George Bataille (1897–1962). The resurgence of interest in his writing in the 1980s and 1990s—specifically through the categories of horizontality, base materialism, pulsation, and entropy that art historians Rosalind Krauss and Yve-Alain Bois developed in their 1997 exhibition catalogue *Formless: A User's Guide*—influenced Black when she was a student. [5] The decomposing powdered structures and goopy, sagging forms that populate her sculpture are certainly receptive to this reading.

While she acknowledges this theoretical precedent, the critical narrative she invokes is Kleinian psychoanalysis, analyst Melanie Klein's theories of human psychological development rooted in the relationship between mother and infant. It is with Melanie Klein's focus on artistic creativity that Black closely aligns her own production as an artist, and where her physical "repression" of materials finds a psychological metaphor.

Like Bataille's, Melanie Klein's work experienced a surge in popularity within academia in the 1990s. Klein (1882-1960) is credited with having radically shifted Freudian analysis from a conversation-based "talking-cure" for adults to the realm of early childhood by allowing play to stand for language as a form of free association in therapy. Providing toys and artistic materials like glue and paint during sessions, she both observed and communicated with her young patients as they actively engaged with the environment of her office. As children drew and painted pictures, built cities of blocks, and sometimes destroyed these constructions in outbursts of violence, the floor of Klein's office became the site for acts of creativity. Black has spoken about her focus on horizontality, rooted in walking the Scottish countryside, head down, following the textures and contours of the earth; of her fascination with children's play; and how these interests translate to her practice. The ground is often the origin of human creativity, the location in which most children first draw with fingers in spills of water and milk or shape sand and dirt with their hands.[6] Our earliest artistic experiences are with these basic, banal materials, though our intimate relationship with the ground fades as we learn to walk. At one point Black declared that she would never make an object that could stand on its own, and many of her works struggle to reach an upright position. Her current sculptural forms continue to demonstrate a failure to resist the pull of gravity, and the materials chosen are often unable to withstand this force for the duration of their display. Powders crumble, liquids ooze, and the occasional piece of cellophane falls to be left where it lands.

Significantly, the paint Black uses to cover wide expanses of gallery floors is sourced from a children's art supply store in the UK. Mixed with plaster powder to specific pastel shades and sifted, spread, or molded into shapes, these large-scale geometric objects often resemble simple childhood toys, such as blocks, and lend a playroom quality to certain sculptures. Black's own fascination with powdery substances can be traced to her childhood through her mother's recollection that she loved handling flour and sugar in the kitchen as a little girl. Her taste in color is equally imbued with personal history—her recollection of her grandmother's cakes, for instance. Black has stated repeatedly that she chooses colors she likes, colors that she wants to see for extended periods, and she likes pink: "It's hard enough to make something that's any good, so you may as well start with some sort of self-indulgence."[7] Though Black deflects the gendered readings of color in her work, the use of pastels does allude to childhood for many viewers: "baby blues" and "bubblegum pinks" dominate children's clothing and toys, and the use of these shades amplifies the feeling of play within the work.

Practically In Shadow was one of Black's most colorful works. She responded to ICA's towering vertical space with a major, multi-part sculpture incorporating her largest hanging polythene object to date. Black used polythene—the common plastic of disposable shopping bags and food cartons—in thin sheets, attracted to its paper-like quality, and she prefers the term "plastic" be avoided to maintain the allusion to paper. Suspended among skylights, this pale pink and blue prismatic structure was continuously transformed through shifts in natural light, gently undulating with the flow of air. The floor element of the work amassed nearly 7,000 pounds of powdered plaster and paint laced with chunks of delicately hued "bath bombs," scented balls of sodium bicarbonate and citric acid that fizz when placed in water (Black's are from the UK-based company that invented them). In signature pastel hues, soft greens and yellows swelled across the landscape of the gallery into a raised hill caked with powder, marking the edge of the pale blue rectangular floor structure. In an adjacent corner a large, multi-layered confection of pink and white powder compressed almost into a cube, crowned by a circular cellophane form, was left to crumble over the course of the exhibition.

Practically In Shadow dwarfs the viewer. (There is an *Alice In Wonderland* shift in scale as one enters the gallery.) The bath bombs permeate the space—full of large candy-hued shapes—with a floral, almost sugary scent, while the polythene clouds recall bundles of cotton candy. Young children experience the world through taste as well as touch, and these sculptures play on a primal desire to lick—to taste as a form of knowledge—that adults have been conditioned to resist. Black's work celebrates these urges, and the unconscious decisions and physical movements an artist makes while immersed in her chosen materials. Her hope is to elicit an equally visceral response from viewers. The desire to touch her sculptures can often be overpowering, a desire the artist courts. The institutional prohibitions against touching a work of art create a tension that amplifies its materiality, an experience that Black views as outside of language. Citing Melanie Klein's recognition of physical movement—through creativity and play—as a valid form of communication, Black roots much of her creative process in a state of pre-language.

This mild logophobia extends to the institutional context of each sculpture. As museums venture further into heavy didactics—with audio tours, iPad apps, and ever lengthening wall labels—Black continues to resist the intrusion of text into the space of her sculptures. The walls of the gallery are left blank, and museum didactics are placed outside the entrance. Suspicion of language, of the way it dominates how art is experienced, has instilled in Black a need for a heightened level of control in how her work circulates through the critical receptors of the art world, to guide the language that surrounds her practice. A talented writer with a graduate degree in Philosophy, her contributions to catalogues and gallery press releases have successfully reified certain terms and phrases while censoring others. The works are *sculptures* and not *installations*. They are *polythene*, not *plastic*. She uses powdered *paint*, not *pigment*, the latter being too closely aligned with painting. As a young artist Black understood the way language is regenerated by curators and critics—its textual diaspora—and quite early in her career set linguistic parameters for her work's reception.

Black's working method is intensely physical and ideally solitary. That she is alone in the gallery for days, even weeks, to produce these sculptures is essential. She describes her connection to the work as instinctive, and although her individual labor is not always explicitly evident in the finished sculpture, the act of moving and shaping these materials herself is at the core of her practice. The increasing scale of the projects she is creating for institutions, principally museum spaces, is what she has always envisioned in terms of size and scope: the work can now "become what it was always meant to be." Only recently, and reluctantly, has she allowed any assistance in making these works, enlisting her brother and sister-in-law in the creation of *Practically In Shadow*. Physical exhaustion complicates her ability to think through the most intricate aesthetic decisions during the final days of installation. For this reason, engaging assistants during the early, more physically laborious stages has been a necessary addition to what is essentially a private, meditative process.

Working with these materials is also a working through: there is the investment of emotional labor. Intimate understanding of materials—as Black intimately understands the weight and texture of the materials she uses, how they dry or cake—is a central component of psychoanalyst Hanna Segal's focus on artistic production.[8] Segal (1918-2011) expanded Melanie Klein's minimal writing on aesthetics and theorized that depressive anxiety is alleviated in creative people through the production of works of art. Within the Kleinian framework, the relationship between mother and child during infancy is the most significant stage in psychological development, eclipsing Freud's phallic and father-centered Oedipal stage with one in which the child traumatically learns that its mother is a separate subject. This initial state of loss, and the process of mourning that the child undergoes to recover, is repeated throughout one's life as we lose—through death or estrangement—those we love. For Segal, the cycle of loss and mourning is an essential and unavoidable human experience, and is at the core of all creativity. An artist's ability to work through the mourning process is directly related to the aesthetic success of the work of art. Black aligns herself with these aspects of Kleinian aesthetic theory, viewing artistic production as a psychological release rooted in mourning.[9] The joy, frustration, and aggression that are harnessed to make her sculptures are part of this process, one that plays out both consciously and unconsciously in the mind of the artist.

Though Black's work seems to embrace, even revel, in process, she is more concerned with the aesthetic object produced—the "aesthetic by-product," as she has referred to her finished sculptures. There is a period of "loose experimentation" in the early stages of installation. The topography of her environmentally scaled work is roughly pre-determined, and colors and dimensions are tentatively set before installation begins. During the final stages of this process Black is alone in the gallery and focuses on the minuscule formations within the sculpture. Her hands mark certain works more visibly than others. A kind of signature without letters, these impressions suggest the presence of the artist in the physical creation of the sculpture: using fingers to make indentations along the edges of powdered floor structures, or dusting chalk on her hands before manipulating transparent or sticky materials like polythene and adhesive tape—marks to be discovered by observant viewers as nearly imperceptible fingerprints. She has written about her interest in early human mark-making, the handprints and scratches found in caves, forms of creativity that predate language.[10] Though Black avoids figurative imagery in her sculptures, the body is present as a tool: mixing and spreading powder, forming the cellophane. Like these early forms of human visual communication, her bodily prints mark these massive forms as handmade objects.

The moment Black decides the sculpture is done is the moment it begins to unravel. Gravity, the flow of air, light, and the gallery's temperature all affect the substances Black uses. Though these works may be materially unstable, they are collectible. Each sculpture can potentially be remade by the artist. Some elements can be stored and conserved while other materials—such as the powders and cosmetics—need to be refreshed. Her sculptures are infinitely regenerative, and what they complicate is our notion of permanence, both of a work of art and of the body. The skin-like membranes of polythene coated with chalk and make-up, the bath bombs gradually disintegrating into dust—these are the creams and lotions we use to delay and mask the decay of our own bodies. There is an evocation of flesh in these materials, intensified by the gently pulsating grids that hang within *Practically In Shadow*. These colorful substances are pleasurable to look at and, we assume, were pleasurable for the artist to handle. As they inevitably dry and discolor—into a kind of desiccated, caking goo—they heighten our sense as viewers that this work is temporally bound to its materials.

Though Black uses many traditional artistic materials, they are incorporated in a "pre-object" or "post-object" state. Plaster powder and powdered paint link her work to sculpture and painting— threads of nail polish poured onto the floor of *Practically In Shadow* cleverly nod to Pollack's drips—yet her work resists the dominant traditions of each. In the final stages of the work's creation, Black will ask herself if what she has made could qualify as a good painting. If the answer is yes, the work is finished. This work straddles an extreme verticality and expansive horizontality, the axis of painting and sculpture. ICA's Second Floor Space offers a ceiling height that rivals that of any of Black's previous installation sites. She frequently responds to high, light-filled spaces with web-like hanging structures, such as *Necessity* (2012) recently commissioned for the large atrium windows of the Dallas Museum of Art. Like the polythene used in ICA's gallery, these fence-like formations droop due to their material conditions, alluding, if reluctantly, to the grid.

Black's grid is a flaccid structure, impotent as a useful demarcation of space, but with allusions to De Stijl and the Bauhaus, and to the soft geometry of Jasper Johns and Agnes Martin. Grids, as Rosalind Krauss argued in her 1979 essay, are anti-narrative.[11] They exclude language from entering the artwork, and allow a basis in materialism—in the physical substance of the work—while gesturing towards the immaterial.[12] Even the inchoate, sagging grids of Black's works signal this dual nature. She wants to lose herself in the process of making but produce a successful aesthetic object. She wants the sculptures to remain unchanged but insists on using unstable materials. She wants to have her cake and eat it, too.

1 In numerous interviews, Black references the "almost," "only just," and "not quite." See, for example, Ana Finel Honigman, "Karla Black in Conversation," *Sculpture* (July 2010) and Andrew Cattanach, "Karla Black – Her Dark Materials," *The Skinny* (June 2011).

2 Karla Black, email message to author, April 1, 2013.

3 Robert Morris, "Anti Form," *Artforum* (April 1968): 35.

4 "Recently I have taken the formless materials through a process of tentative repression, and have been concentrating, through very specific colours and qualities of surface, on the level of attractiveness in the various sculptures made." Karla Black quoted in a 2008 press release from Galerie Gisela Capitain.

5 Yve-Alain Bois and Rosalind Krauss, *Formless: A User's Guide*, (Cambridge: MIT Press,1997).

6 Conversation with the artist, April 2013.

7 Karla Black, "500 Words," *Artforum* online, October 13, 2009: http://artforum.com/words/id-23949.

8 Hanna Segal, "A Psychoanalytical Approach to Aesthetics," *International Journal of Psychoanalysis* 23 (1952).

9 This "psychological release" is specifically Kleinian reparation, the process by which a subject atones for the destructive impulses directed at loved ones by recreating them symbolically.

10 Karla Black, "It's Proof That Counts," *It's Proof That Counts*, (Zurich: JRP Ringier, 2010):166.

11 Rosalind Krauss, "Grids," *October*, Vol. 9 (Summer, 1979): 50.

12 Ibid. 54.

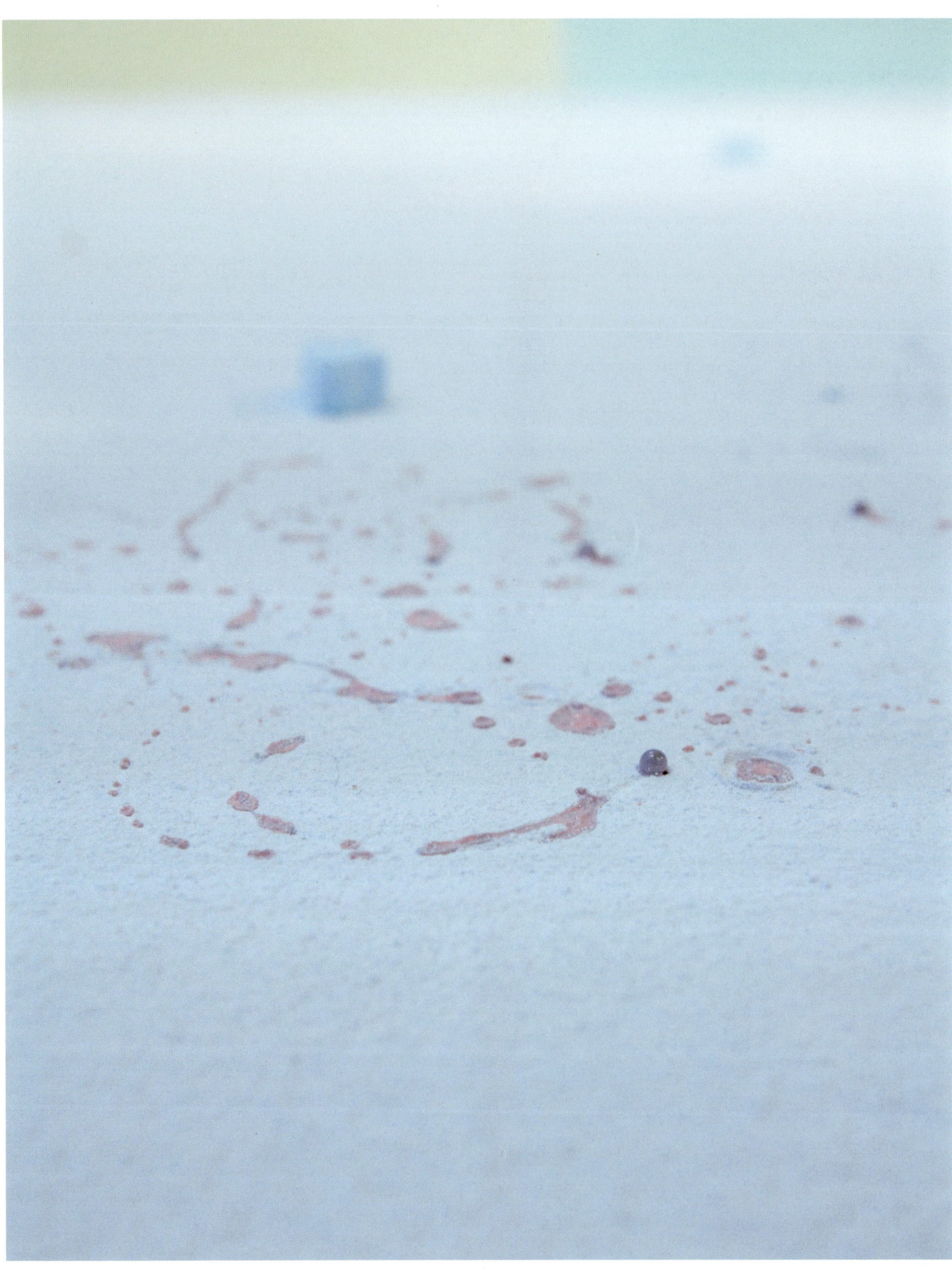

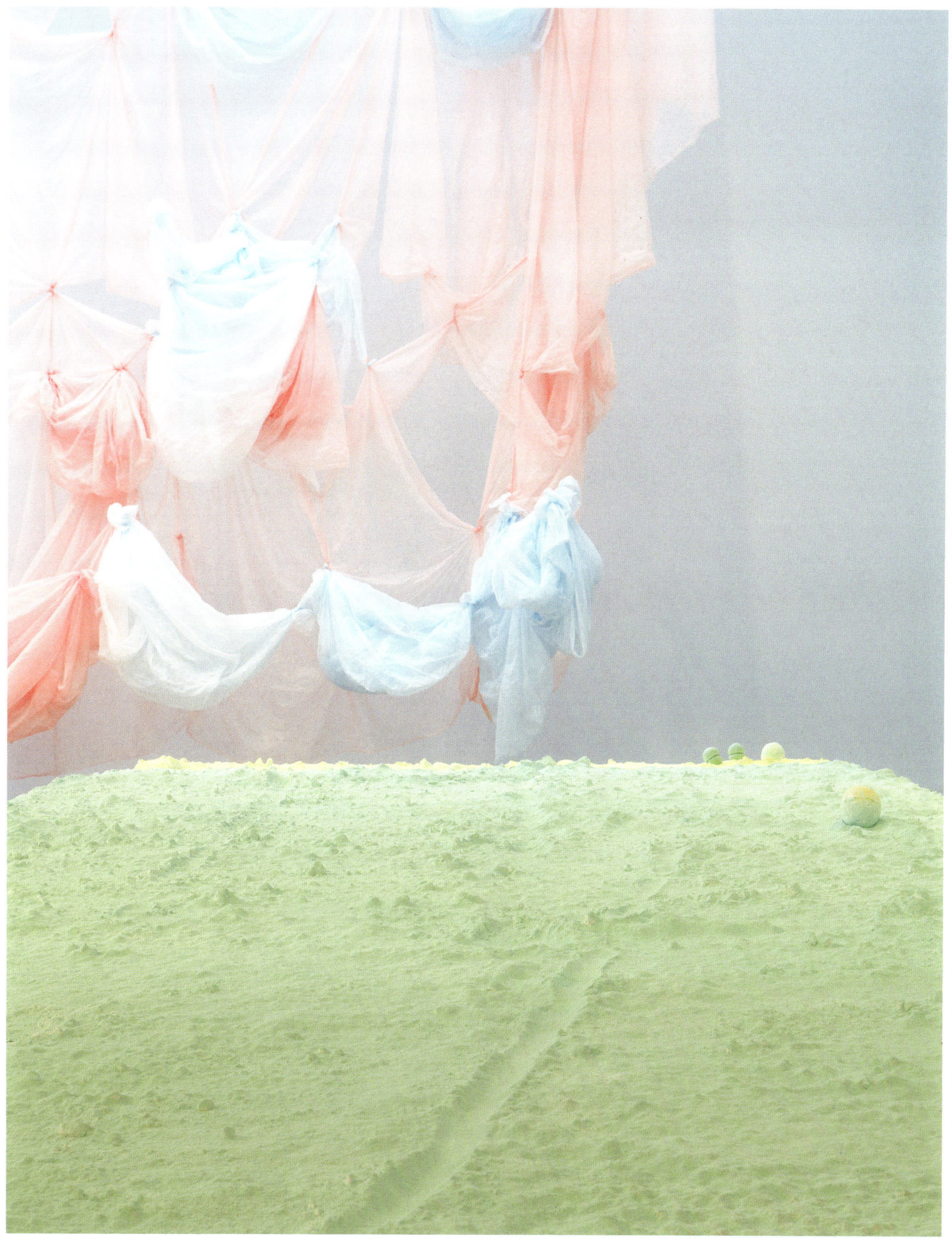

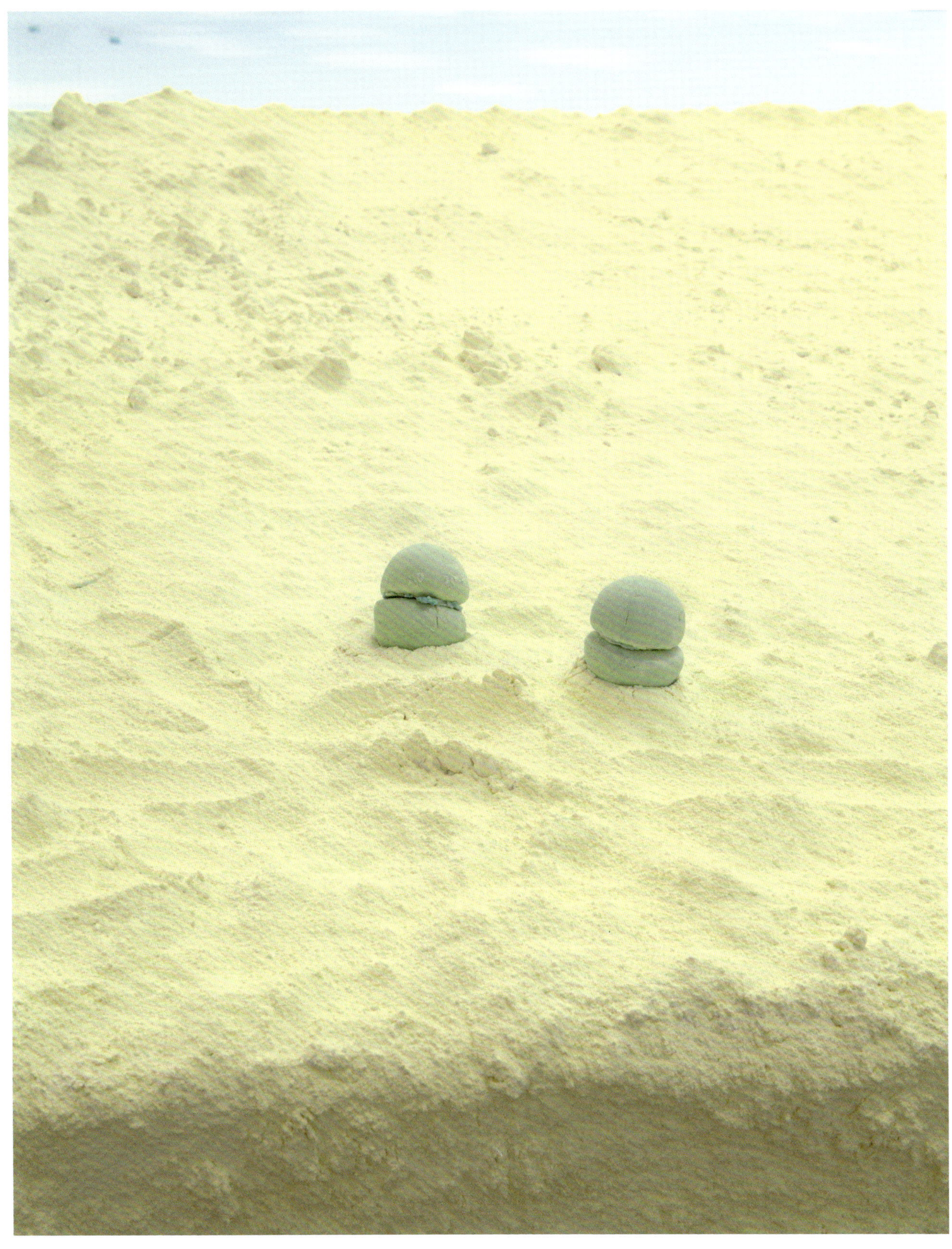

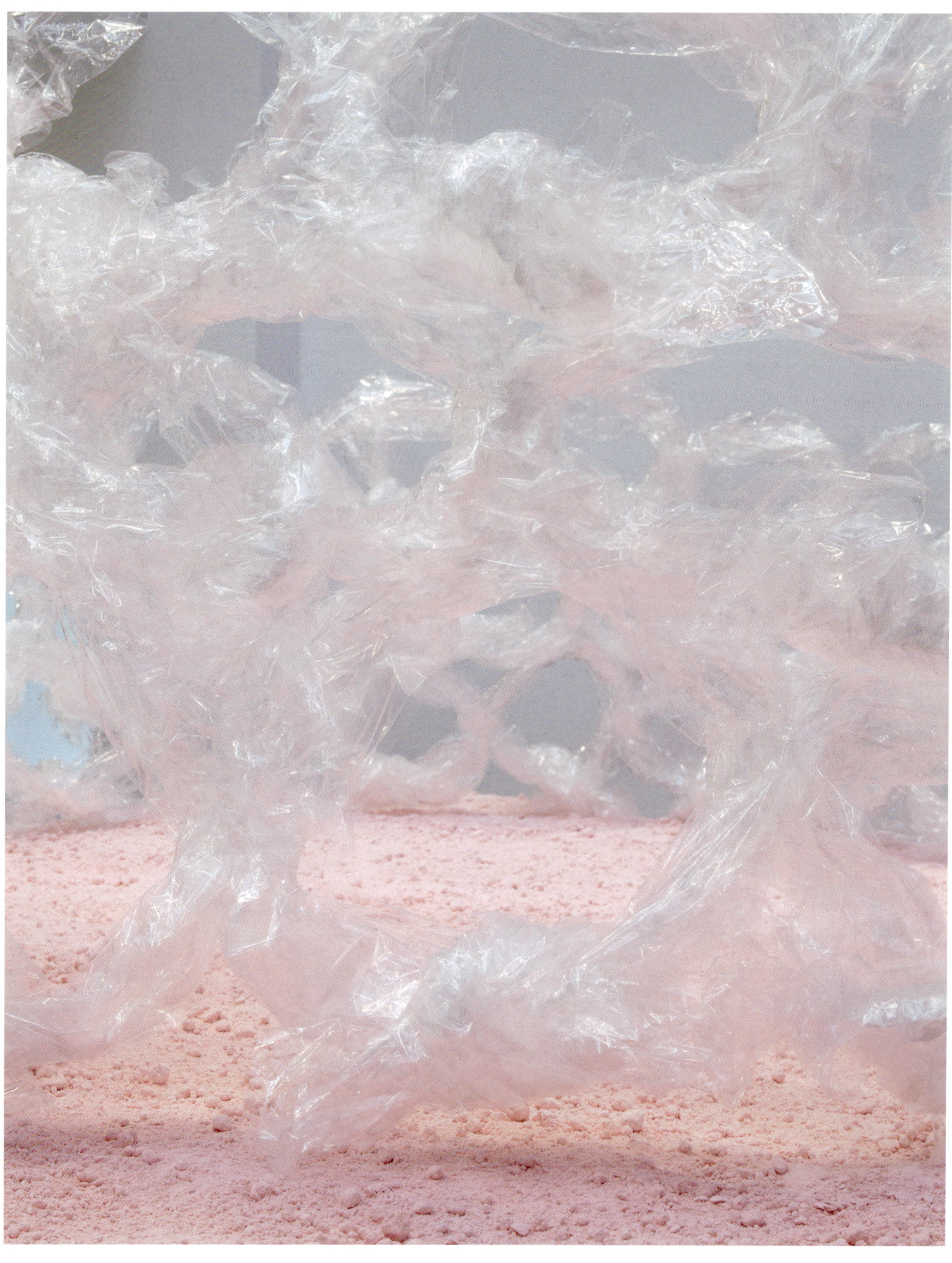

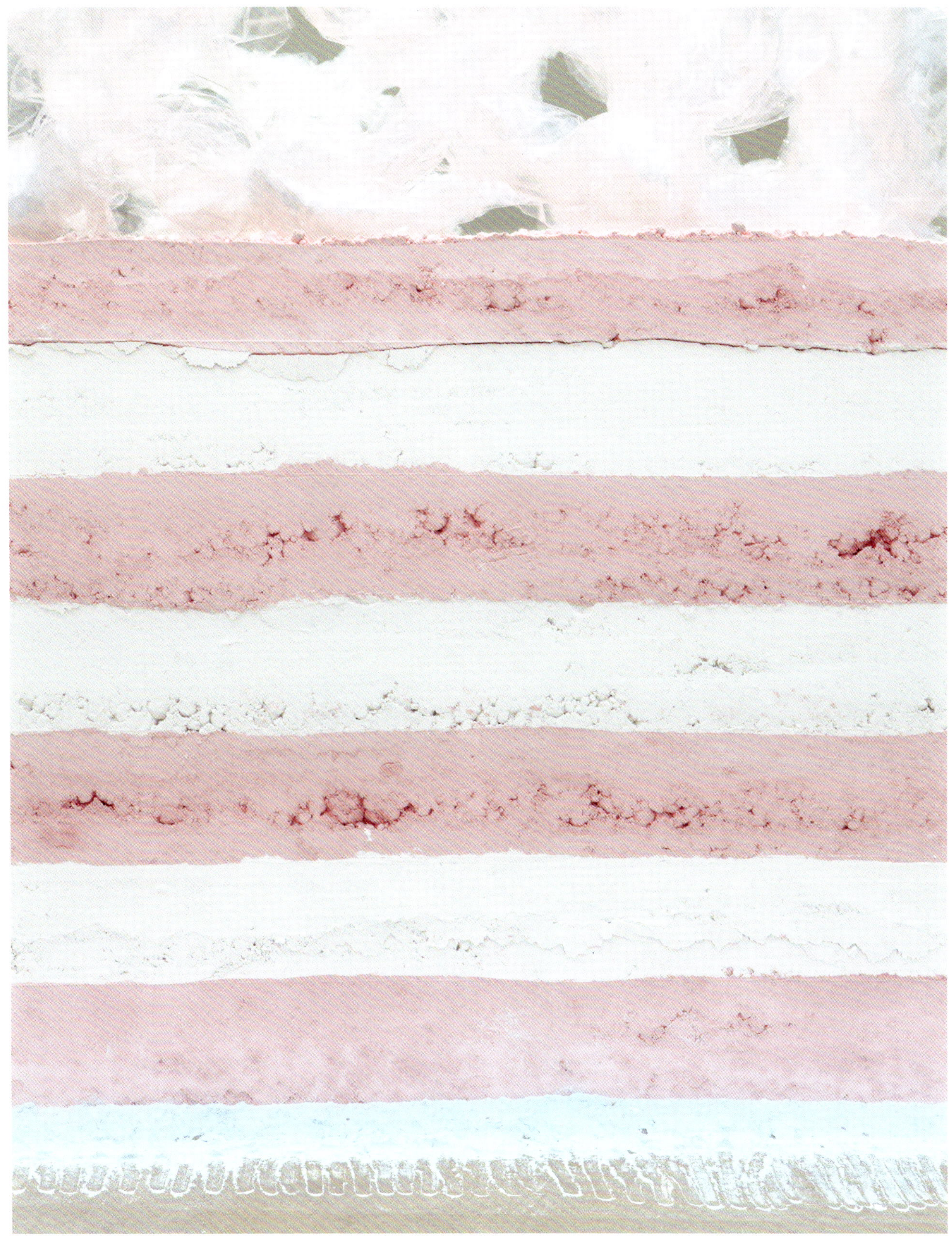

KARLA BLACK

Organized by Kate Kraczon
April 24 – July 28, 2013
Institute of Contemporary Art at the University of Pennsylvania
118 S. 36th St. Philadelphia, PA 19104-3289

Exhibition funding has been provided by Julie L. & Lawrence J. Bernstein; Carol T. & John G. Finley; Kirk Kirkpatrick; Marjorie E. & Michael J. Levine; and Josephine M. and Christopher C. Schlank.

Publications including exhibition catalogs are supported by an endowment from Barbara B. & Theodore R. Aronson.

Programming associated with this exhibition has been made possible in part by the Emily and Jerry Spiegel Fund to Support Contemporary Culture and Visual Arts and the Lise Spiegel Wilks and Jeffrey Wilks Family Foundation; and by Hilarie L. and Mitchell Morgan.

Additional funding has been provided by the Horace W. Goldsmith Foundation; the Dietrich Foundation, Inc.; the Overseers Board for the Institute of Contemporary Art; friends and members of ICA; and the University of Pennsylvania. Free admission to ICA for the public is sponsored by the Amanda (C95) & Glenn (W87/WG88) Fuhrman Fund. Marketing is supported by Lisa A. and Stephen A. Tananbaum. General operating support provided, in part, by the Philadelphia Cultural Fund and the Barra Foundation. ICA receives state arts funding support through a grant from the Pennsylvania Council on the Arts, a state agency funded by the Commonwealth of Pennsylvania and the National Endowment for the Arts, a federal agency. ICA thanks La Colombe for providing complimentary coffee at public events. ICA acknowledges Le Méridien Philadelphia as our official Unlock Art™ partner hotel.

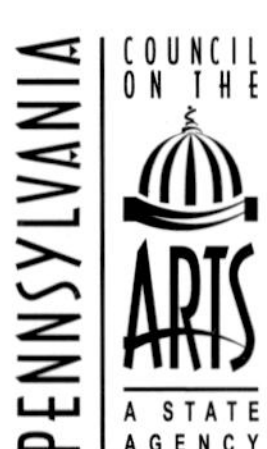
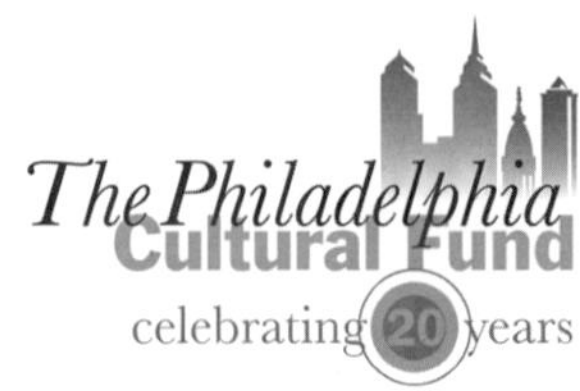

ICA Staff

ICA Board of Overseers

ICA Student Advisory Council

ISBN: 978-0-88454-128-8